The Brilliant Bassoon

Music Theory Book 1

A theory book especially for bassoonists

All the basics to get you going.
Easy to follow explanations,
puzzles and more. All with the
beginner bassoonist in mind.

Amanda Oosthuizen

Jemima Oosthuizen

The Brilliant Bassoon Series
Wild Music Publications
www.wildmusicpublications.com

CW00507269

We hope you enjoy *The Brilliant Bassoon Music Theory Book 1*.

Take a look at our other exciting books, including: 50+ Greatest Classics, Catch the Beat, Christmas Duets, Easy Tunes from Around the World, Trick or Treat – A Halloween Suite, Champagne and Chocolate, and many more solo and duet books.

For more info on other amazing books, please go to:

WildMusicPublications.com

For a **free stuff** and for the **answer booklet** visit our **secret bassoon page**:

http://WildMusicPublications.com/**secret32-bassoon-track12/**

And use the password: **BSNtrack4U**

Happy Music Making!

The Wild Music Publications Team

To keep up –to-date with our new releases, why not **follow us on Twitter**

@WMPublications

To play the bassoon well, you need to read music and understand the mysteries of music theory. The Brilliant Bassoon Music Theory Book 1 includes all the basics you'll need up to Grade 2 bassoon and is written with the beginner bassoonist in mind. Take it slowly, complete a little bit at a time and have fun!

Each section explains a new aspect of music in an easy-to-read way and is followed by exercises and puzzles to help you remember what you've learnt.

Writing activities are shown by a bassoon pencil.

After several sections, you will find a Check page where you can see how much you have remembered and keep score.

At the end of the book, there are bassoon information pages, more puzzles, a list of musical terms and symbols and a chart where you can keep a record of the sections you have completed.

If you want to check your **ANSWERS**, a free answer book download is available on the **SECRET BASSOON PAGE** of our website. Find out how to get there on the second page of the book.

When you have finished, take a look at Book 2. It includes all the crazy theory you need to know from Grades 3 – 5 bassoon including: tenor clef, ornaments, more bassoon facts, making scales, compound time signatures and much more.

Contents

Bass Clef

Bassoon music is mostly written in bass clef.

Bass clef is also called F clef.

Music is written on five lines called a stave (or staff).

The bass clef is drawn at the start of every stave.

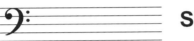 **Stave**

Music is divided into bars by bar lines.

Draw a bass clef in every bar. The two dots always go above and below the F line.

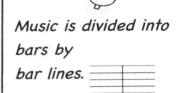

Remember to draw the two dots

The end of a section of music is shown by a double bar line.

The end of a piece of music is shown by a final bar line.

A phrase is a short section of music that makes sense, rather like a sentence.

Phrases are shown by a large slur.

Phrases are often four bars long.

Phrase

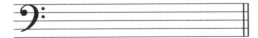

Letter Names

Notes are written on the lines and in the spaces.

The lower sounds are at the bottom of the stave.

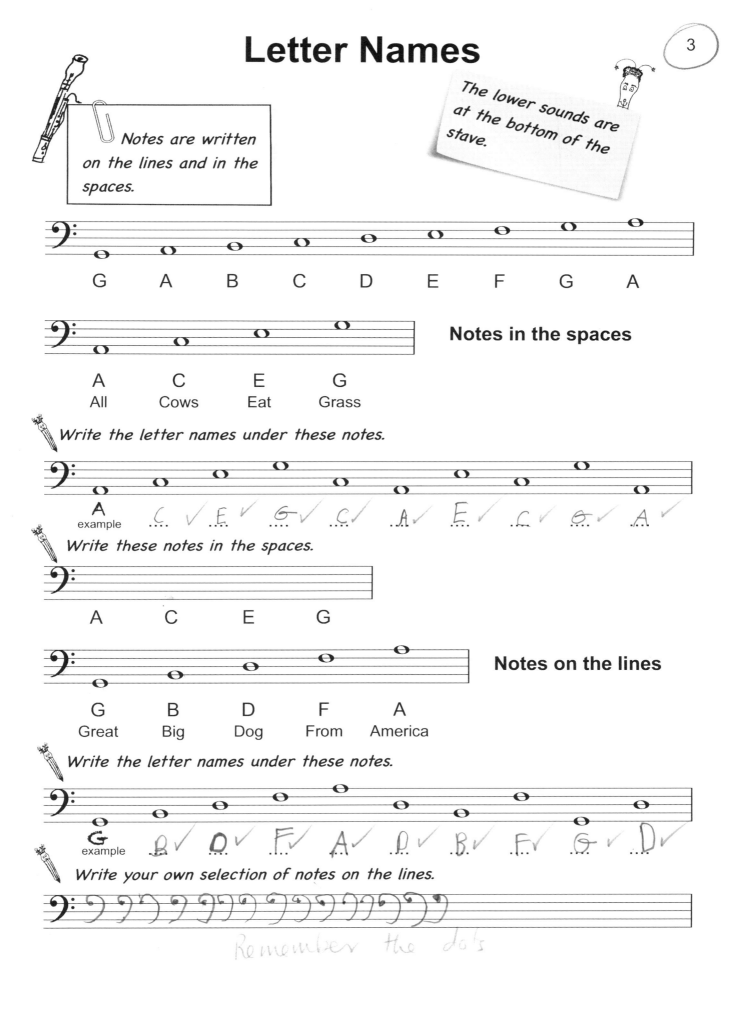

G A B C D E F G A

Notes in the spaces

A C E G
All Cows Eat Grass

Write the letter names under these notes.

A example C E G C A E C G A

Write these notes in the spaces.

A C E G

Notes on the lines

G B D F A
Great Big Dog From America

Write the letter names under these notes.

G example B D F A D B F G D

Write your own selection of notes on the lines.

Remember the do's

4

Write the letter names under these notes in the spaces.

A
example G   ....

Write the letter names under these notes on the lines.

B
example ....

Write your own selection of notes on lines and in spaces.

This line →

Write the letter names under these notes on lines and in spaces.

....

....

....

This line →

....

Write the notes in spaces above the letter names.

example

A   E   C   G   A   E   A   C   E   G

Write the notes on lines above the letter names.

example

B   A   G   B   F   D   G   A   D   F

Write the notes on lines or spaces above the letter names.

example

A   B   C   D   E   F   G   A   G   F   E   D

example

C   B   A   G   B   D   F   A   G   E   C   A

Write notes in lines and spaces starting from the bottom of the stave.

Write the letter names beneath the notes.

B
example ....

....

C
example ....

....

6

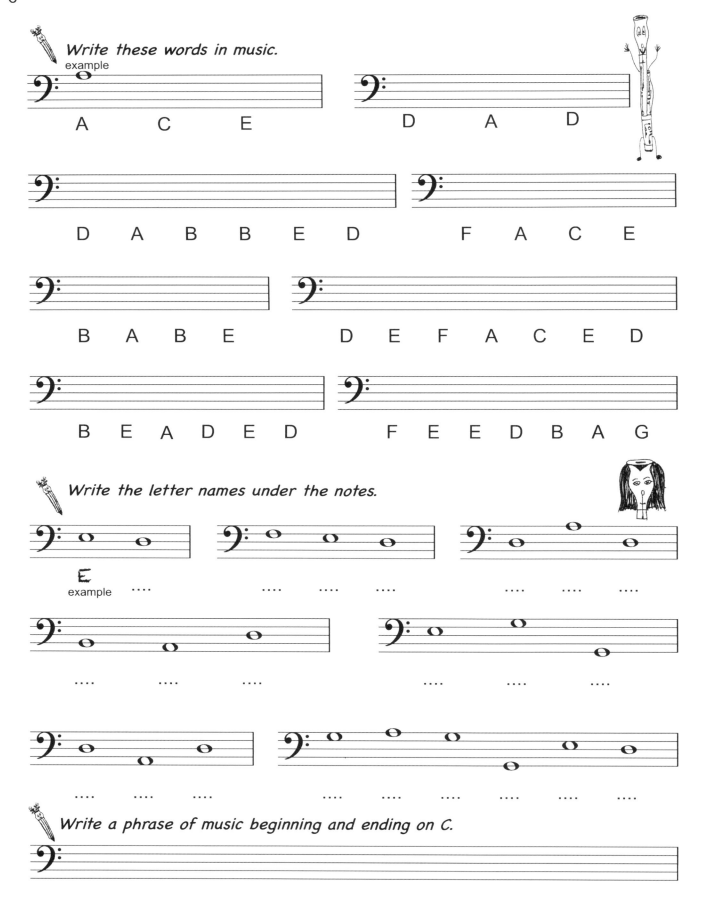

Write these words in music.

example

A   C   E

D   A   D

D A B B E D

F   A   C   E

B   A   B   E

D E F A C E D

B E A D E D

F E E D B A G

Write the letter names under the notes.

E
example   ....

....

....

Write a phrase of music beginning and ending on C.

Note Values

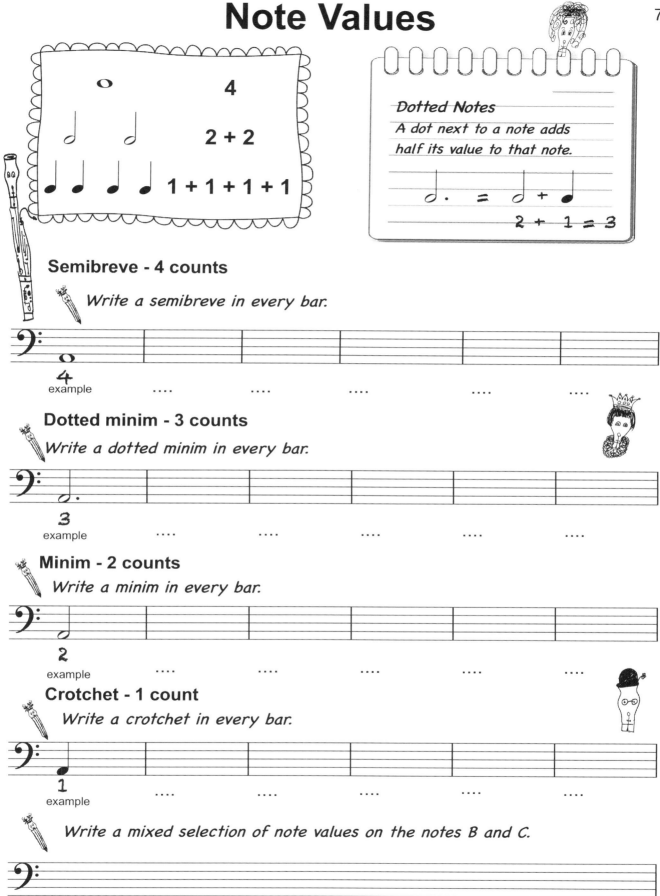

Semibreve - 4 counts

Write a semibreve in every bar.

example

Dotted minim - 3 counts

Write a dotted minim in every bar.

example

Minim - 2 counts

Write a minim in every bar.

example

Crotchet - 1 count

Write a crotchet in every bar.

example

Write a mixed selection of note values on the notes B and C.

Dotted Notes

A dot next to a note adds half its value to that note.

2 + 1 = 3

Write the number of counts.

2
example ....

Ties

A tie is a loop joining notes that are the same. It means add the notes together.

= 2 + 3

Write the counts and do the sum.

2 + 1 = 3
....
example

.... + ... = ...

.... + ... = ...

.... + ... + ... = ...

.... + ... + ... = ...

.... + ... = ...

.... + ... = ...

Write the missing notes below the *.

*

3 counts

*

9 counts

*

5 counts

Write notes that make each bar add up to four crotchets.

Write notes that make each bar add up to three crotchets.

Using low G, A, B and C, (all on the stave) write notes of different lengths.

9

 Match the boxes with the correct number of counts.

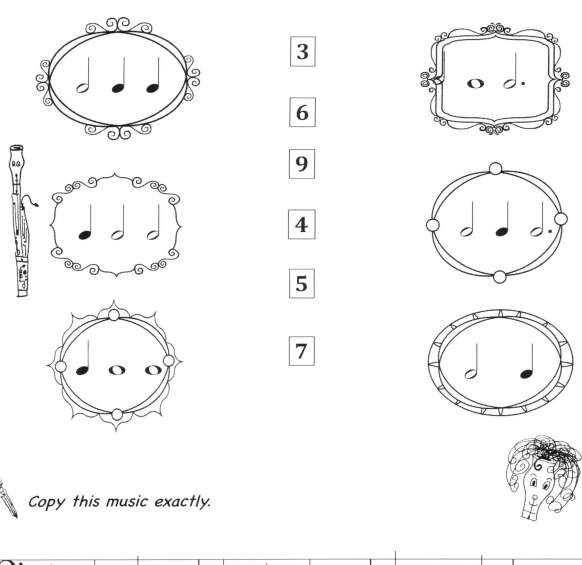

 Copy this music exactly.

Stems

The stems are on the left when they go down.

All notes except semibreves have stems.

The stems are on the right when they go up.

The stem goes down if a note is above the middle line.

The stem goes up if a note is below the middle line.

The stem of D on the middle line can go either up or down.

Add a stem to each of these noteheads.

Write a mixture of low and high noteheads and then add the stems.

Rests

Rests show silence instead of notes.

Semibreve
rest

Also a complete
bar's rest

Minim
rest

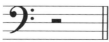

Crotchet
rest

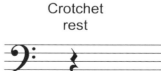

Dotted Minim
rest

2

2 bars rest

164

164 bars rest

 Match the boxes with the correct number of counts.

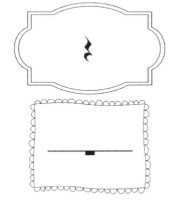

 4

 3

 2

 1

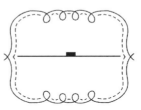

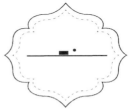

 Draw the rest to match the note.

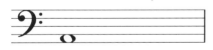

*

*

*

Check 1 Find out how much you remember.

Well done! You have already completed five sections!

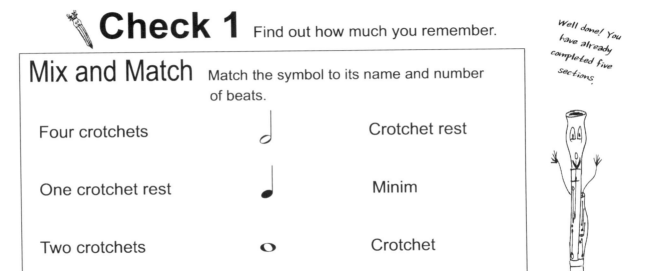

Mix and Match Match the symbol to its name and number of beats.

Four crotchets   Crotchet rest

One crotchet rest   Minim

Two crotchets   Crotchet

One crotchet   Semibreve

Quick Check Are the letters correct. Tick or cross the answers.

G B C E G A F E D A B G C F A A

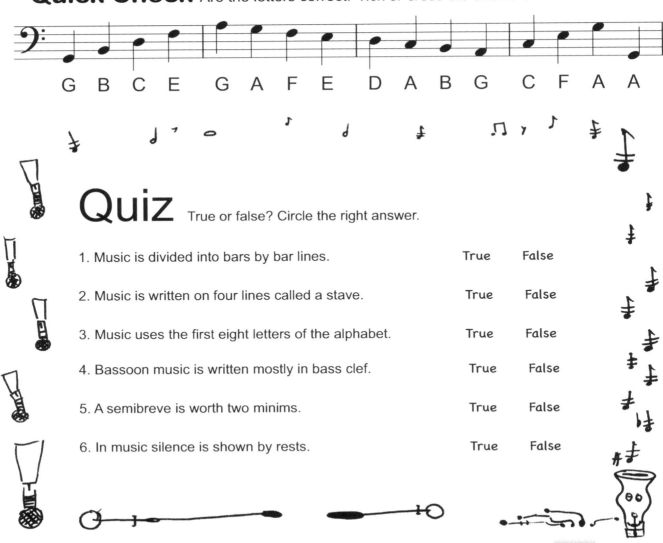

Quiz True or false? Circle the right answer.

1. Music is divided into bars by bar lines.   True   False

2. Music is written on four lines called a stave.   True   False

3. Music uses the first eight letters of the alphabet.   True   False

4. Bassoon music is written mostly in bass clef.   True   False

5. A semibreve is worth two minims.   True   False

6. In music silence is shown by rests.   True   False

How many did you get right?

Time Signatures

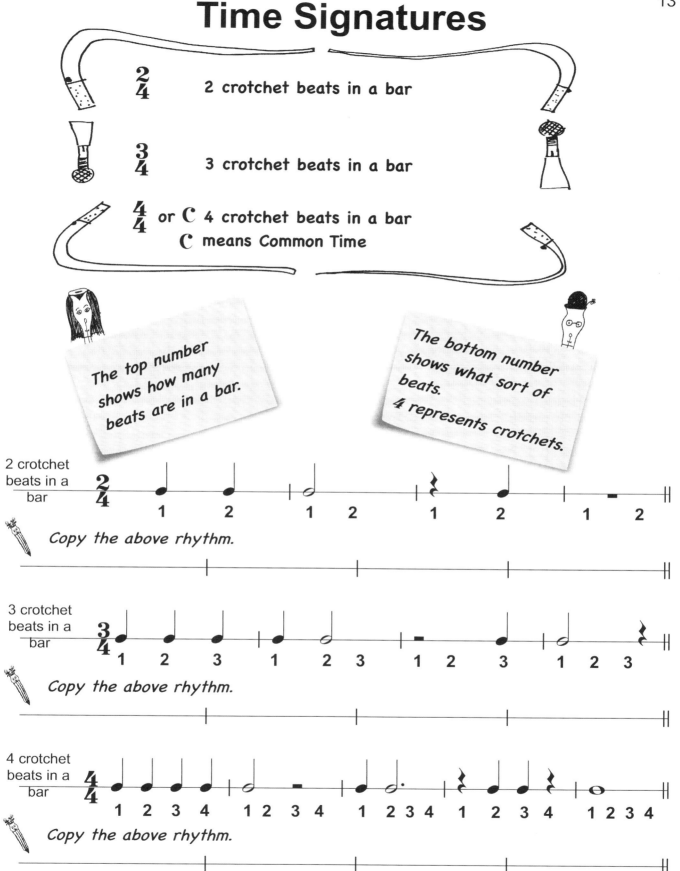

$\frac{2}{4}$ 2 crotchet beats in a bar

$\frac{3}{4}$ 3 crotchet beats in a bar

$\frac{4}{4}$ or C   4 crotchet beats in a bar
        C means Common Time

The top number shows how many beats are in a bar.

The bottom number shows what sort of beats.
4 represents crotchets.

2 crotchet beats in a bar

Copy the above rhythm.

3 crotchet beats in a bar

Copy the above rhythm.

4 crotchet beats in a bar

Copy the above rhythm.

14

Match the bar with its time signature.

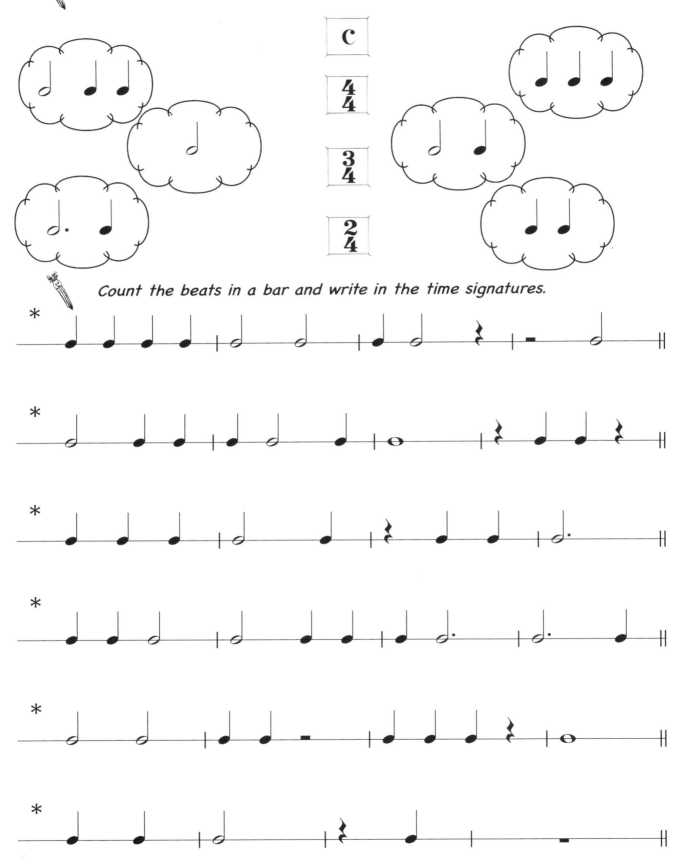

Count the beats in a bar and write in the time signatures.

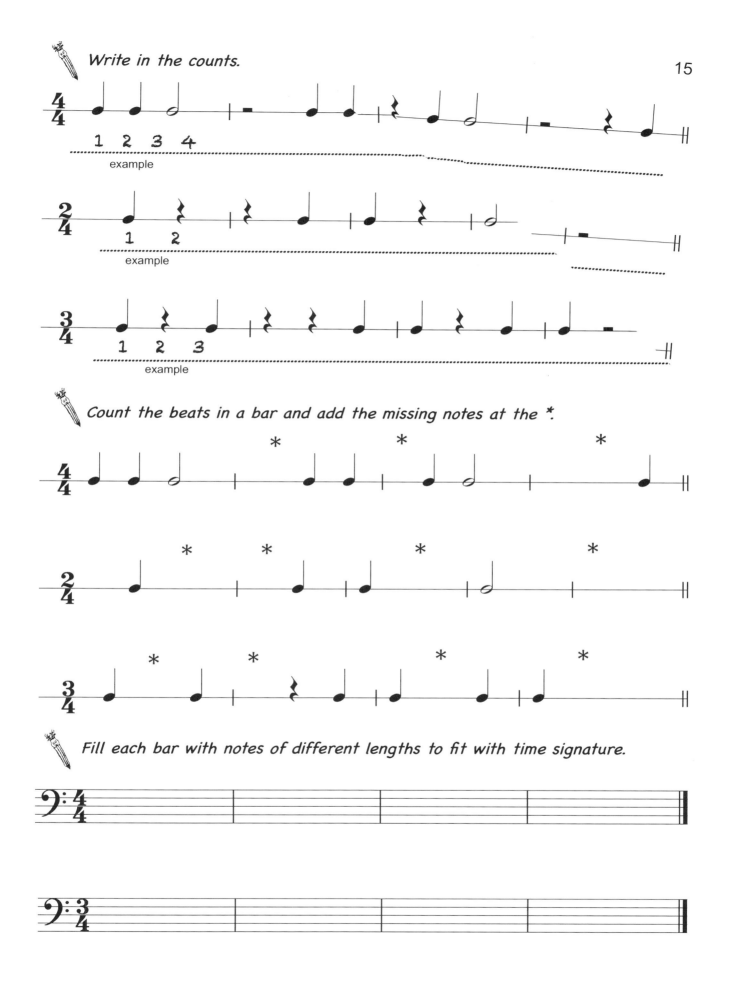

Write in the counts.

15

Count the beats in a bar and add the missing notes at the *.

Fill each bar with notes of different lengths to fit with time signature.

Accidentals

An accidental is a sharp, flat or natural that occurs in a piece of music.

♯ **Sharp** — *A sharp raises a note.*

♭ **Flat** — *A flat lowers a note.*

♮ **Natural** — *A natural restores a note to its original pitch.*

An accidental is written in front of a note.

An accidental changes every following note in the bar that is on the same space or line.

An accidental is written on the same line or in the same space as the note.

Write a sharp before each note.

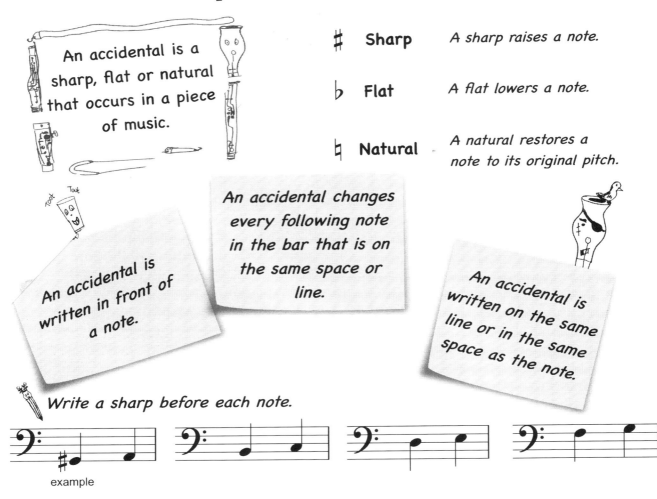

example

Write a flat before each note.

example

Write a natural before each note.

example

Name the notes.

Write the notes.

B♭   F♯   G♯   B♮   E♭   C♯   A♮

G♭   D♮   A♯   E♯   F♭   D♭   C♭

When notes have the same letter name but are different pitches, another accidental is written.

Name the notes.

G♯   G♯
example

Write notes with accidentals but of different lengths so that every bar fits with the time signature.

Quavers

♪ Quaver ♪

𝄾 Quaver rest 𝄾

A quaver is half of one crotchet.

Two quavers are usually beamed together to form a crotchet beat.

The flag is always drawn on the right side of the stem.

2 quavers = 1 crotchet

4 quavers = 1 minim

The first and/or last four quavers in a bar can be beamed together if they form half the bar, but never the middle four.

8 quavers = 1 semibreve

Write groups of quavers and crotchets. Remember to check how many crotchet beats are in a bar.

19

Ledger Lines

✎ Check 2 How much do you remember?

Mix and Match Match the time signature to its description.

Four crotchets in a bar   **2/4**

Three crotchets in a bar   **4/4**

Two crotchets in a bar   **3/4**

Quick Check Are the letter names correct? Tick or cross the answers.

G B♭ C♯ F   C A D A♭   D A E♭ D   C F♭ E♭ A♯

Quiz True or false? Circle the right answer.

1. Two quavers add up to one crotchet.   True   False

2. Four quavers add up to one minim.   True   False

3. A natural sign is not an accidental.   True   False

4. A time signature's top number tells us what sort of beat is in a bar.

True   False

5. A time signature's bottom number tells us what sort of beat is in a bar.

True   False

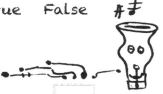

How many did you get right?

Major Scales

All major scales have the same tune based on the steps between notes.

The steps that make up a scale are called tones (whole steps) and semitones (half steps).

Scales are a series of notes going up and down in steps.

All major scales have the same pattern of tones and semitones.

An octave is an interval of eight notes. From low C to high C is an octave.

C major scale (one octave) ascending and descending

tone tone semitone tone tone tone semitone

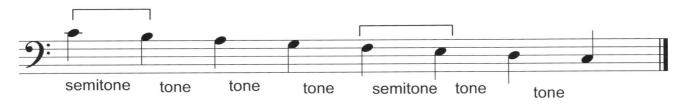

semitone tone tone tone semitone tone tone

Place a bracket above the semitone intervals.

G major scale (one octave) ascending

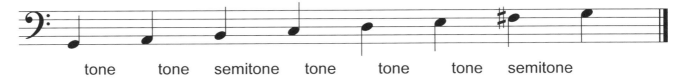

tone tone semitone tone tone tone semitone

F major scale (one octave) ascending

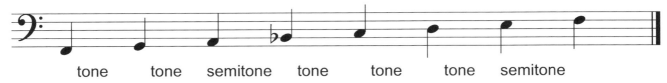

tone tone semitone tone tone tone semitone

✎ *Write in the missing notes and name the scale.*

C ....

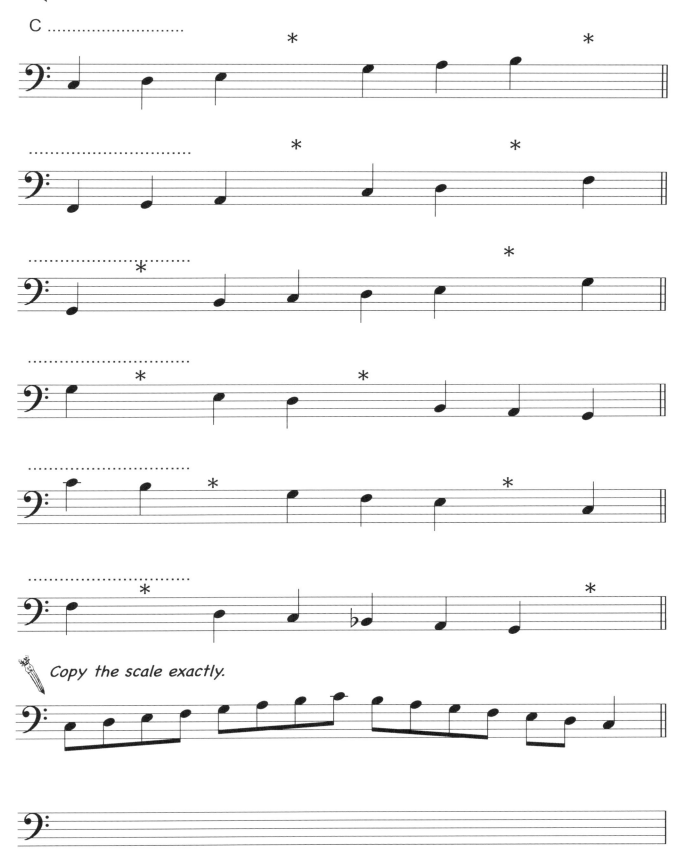

✎ *Copy the scale exactly.*

Key Signatures

Key signatures are sharps or flats at the start of each stave and show which scale is being used in the music.

The key signature of one sharp is always F#.

The key signature of one flat is always B♭.

The key of C major has no sharps or flats.

The key of G major has one sharp, F#.

The key of F major has one flat, B♭.

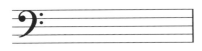

Join the key name to the key signature.

G major

F major

C major

No sharps or flats

F#

B♭

Write the key signatures.

F major

G major

In what key is this phrase? ....

In what key is this phrase? ....

Write the bass clef and the key signature for the scales that start on these notes.

Write the bass clef, the key signature and the scale of F major ascending.

Write the bass clef, the key signature and the scale of G major ascending.

Sometimes the key of a tune or phrase is shown by accidentals, perhaps because it has changed key.

Write the key of this phrase

....

Write the key of this phrase.

....

Write the key of this phrase.

....

Write a phrase in F major that includes accidentals. Start and finish on F.

Dotted Crotchets

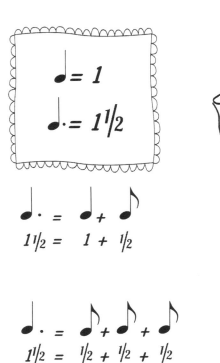

♩ = 1

♩· = 1½

♩· = ♩ + ♪
1½ = 1 + ½

♩· = ♪ + ♪ + ♪
1½ = ½ + ½ + ½

A dot after a note adds half its value to that note.

♩· Dotted crotchet

𝄽· Dotted crotchet rest

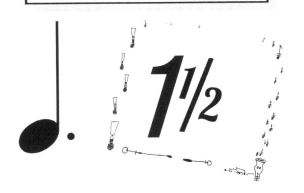

1   2   +   3   4

A dotted crotchet is often followed by a quaver. Together they add up to 2 crotchets.

 Add up the notes and match them to the counts.

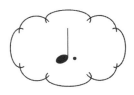   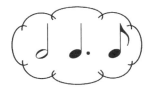      

 | 2 | | 1½ | | 4 |

 Write a dotted crotchet rhythm in each bar.

✎ Write the number of beats in the box.

O = ☐ crotchets

O· = ☐ minims

𝅗𝅥 = ☐ quavers

♩ = ☐ quavers

O· = ☐ crotchets

𝅗𝅥· = ☐ crotchets

♩· = ☐ crotchets

𝅗𝅥· = ☐ quavers

♩· = ☐ quavers

✎ Write in the missing crotchet counts.

1 2 + ...   3 4   1 + ...   +   1   ....

✎ Copy the above tune exactly.

✎ Write a phrase that includes a dotted crotchet rhythm. Begin and end on G.

✎ Write a phrase that includes a dotted crotchet rhythm. Begin and end on C.

28 ✎ Add a dotted note to make each bar the correct length.

Match the note with the
rest of the same length.

Write in the counts.

1 2

Write the scale of G major in dotted crotchets and quavers.

Write the scale of F major in dotted crotchets and quavers.

✎ Check 3 How much do you remember?

Mix and Match Match the scale with its key signature.

C major scale   F♯

G major scale   B♭

F major scale   No ♯ No ♭

Quick Check Are the key signatures correct? Tick or cross the answers.

Cmajor

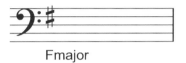

Fmajor

Gmajor

   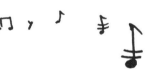

🎵 Quiz True or false? Circle the right answer.

1. A dot next to a note doubles the note in length.   True   False

2. Key signatures are written at the start of a line.   True   False

3. The scale of G major has B flat.   True   False

4. Semitones and tones are steps between notes.   True   False

5. All major scales have different patterns of tones and semitones.

True   False

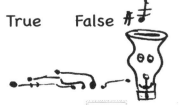

How many did you get right?

Degrees of the Scale

Degrees of the Scale
The first note of a scale is the keynote or 1st degree. The second note is the 2nd degree and the third is the 3rd degree. This contunues until the 8th degree or octave.

So the third degree in C major is the note E.

Degrees of the Scale

C major

1st   2nd   3rd   4th   5th   6th   7th   8th
Keynote   Octave

Write the degree of the scale in the key of C major.

example

3rd   5th   1st   8th

Write the degree of the scale in the key of F major. (F is the 1st degree)

example

8th   4th   6th   2nd

Write the degree of the scale in the key of G major. (G is the 1st degree)

example

2nd   3rd   8th   5th

Write a phrase in C major using only the 1st, 2nd, 3rd and 5th degrees of the scale.

Write a phrase in C major using only the 8th, 6th, 5th and 4th degrees of the scale.

Intervals

Match the interval with its description.

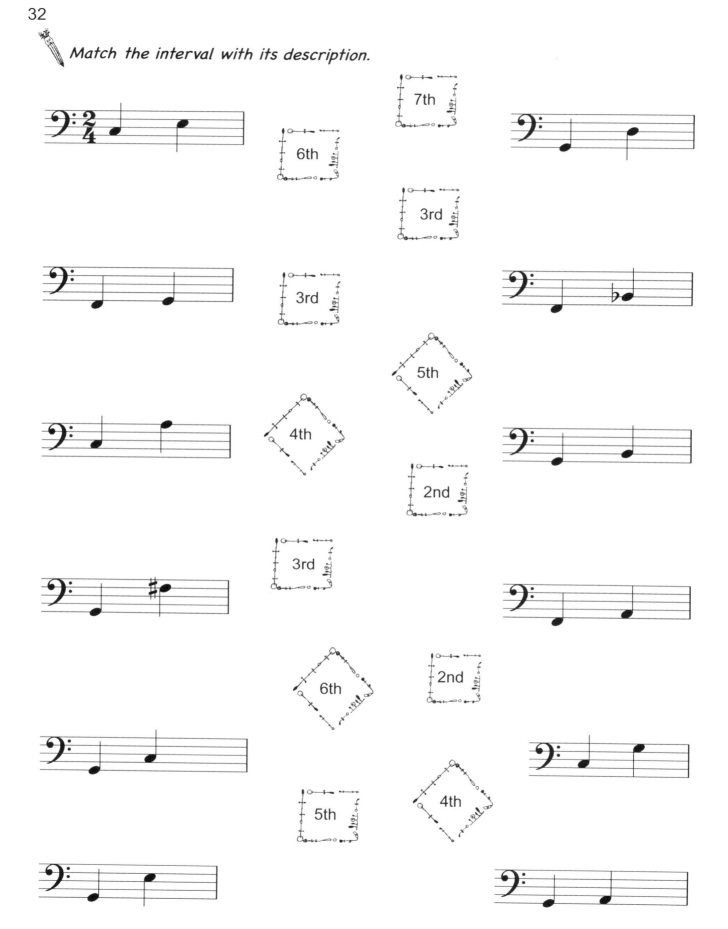

Minor Scales

Relatives
Each minor scale shares a key signature with a major scale. They are related.

The relative minor keynote is the sixth note of the major scale.

There are three kinds of minor scale. They are:
the natural minor scale,
the harmonic minor scale,
the melodic minor scale.
(In Book 2)

In C major, the sixth note of the scale is A. So A minor is the relative minor.

The natural minor scale has exactly the same notes as its relative major. But it starts on the 6th note of the major scale.

A natural minor scale (relative major is C major)

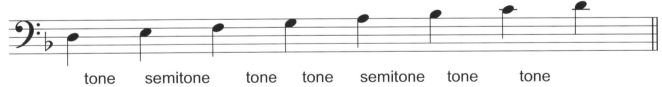

tone   semitone   tone   tone   semitone   tone   tone

Place a bracket above the semitone intervals.

D natural minor scale (relative major is F major)

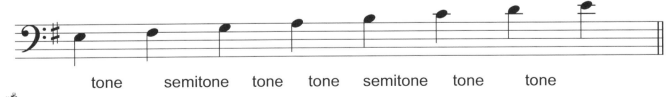

tone   semitone   tone   tone   semitone   tone   tone

Place a bracket above the semitone intervals.

E natural minor scale (relative major is G major)

tone   semitone   tone   tone   semitone   tone   tone

Write a phrase using only the notes of the A natural minor scale. Begin and end on A.

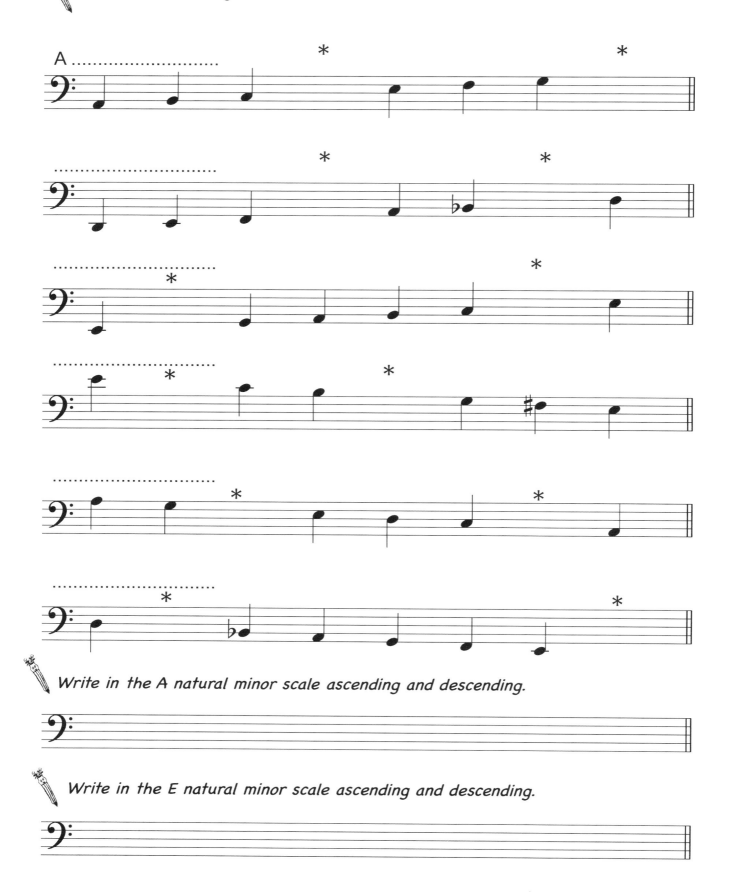

34. Write in the missing notes and name the scale.

Write in the A natural minor scale ascending and descending.

Write in the E natural minor scale ascending and descending.

Pair up the minor key with its key signature and relative major.

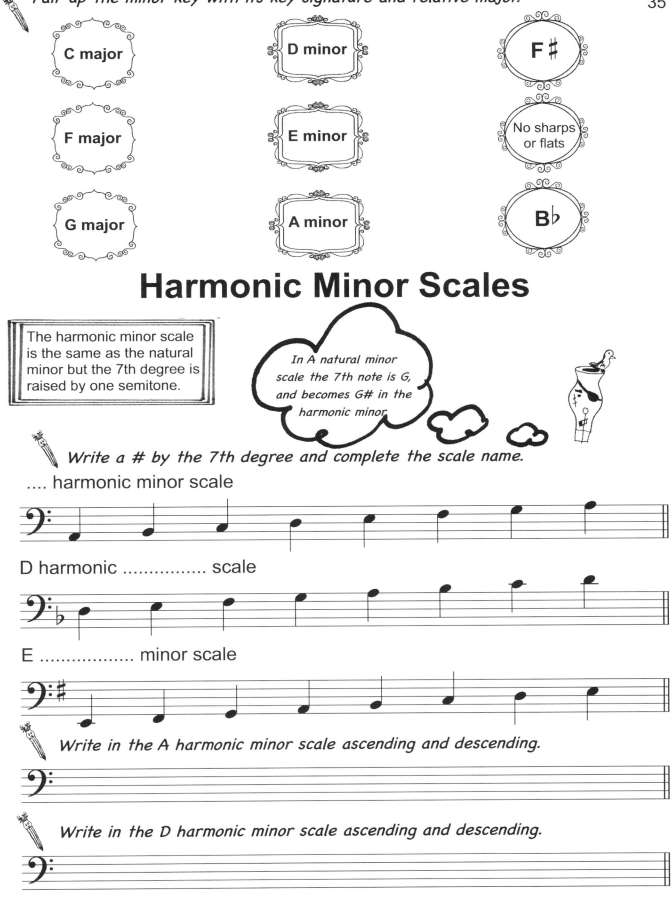

C major

F major

G major

D minor

E minor

A minor

F♯

No sharps or flats

B♭

Harmonic Minor Scales

The harmonic minor scale is the same as the natural minor but the 7th degree is raised by one semitone.

In A natural minor scale the 7th note is G, and becomes G# in the harmonic minor.

Write a # by the 7th degree and complete the scale name.

.... harmonic minor scale

D harmonic .... scale

E .... minor scale

Write in the A harmonic minor scale ascending and descending.

Write in the D harmonic minor scale ascending and descending.

Arpeggios

Arpeggios are made from the 1st, 3rd, 5th and 8th degrees of the scale.

Major and minor arpeggios are made in the same way.

The interval between the 1st and 3rd notes in a minor scale is called a minor 3rd and is made up of three semitones.

C major scale

① ③ ⑤ ⑧

1 2 3 4 5 6 7 8

A natural minor scale

① ③ ⑤ ⑧

1 2 3 4 5 6 7 8

C major arpeggio

major third

A minor arpeggio

minor third

Colour in the notes that form the arpeggios in the scales below.

F major scale

G major scale

Remember to count from the lowest note of the scale.

Colour in the notes that form the arpeggios in the scales below.

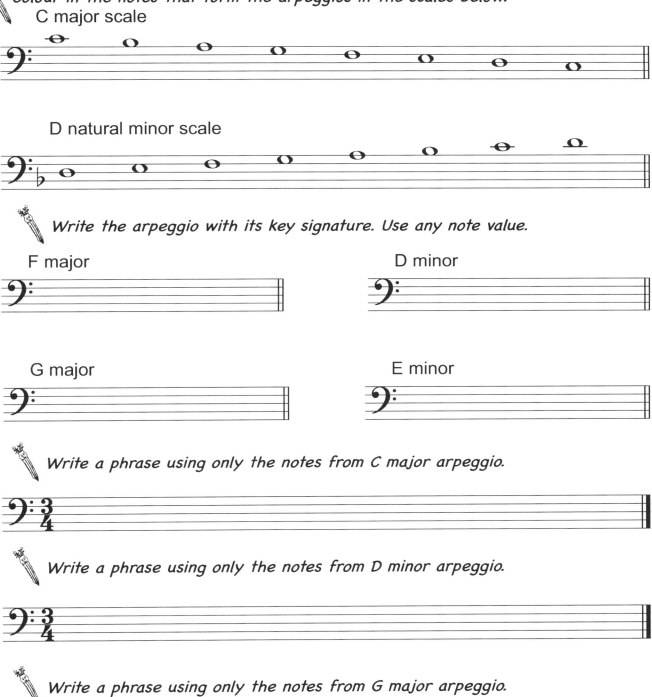

C major scale

D natural minor scale

Write the arpeggio with its key signature. Use any note value.

F major

D minor

G major

E minor

Write a phrase using only the notes from C major arpeggio.

Write a phrase using only the notes from D minor arpeggio.

Write a phrase using only the notes from G major arpeggio.

✏ Check 4 How much do you remember?

Hurray! You're well on your way now.

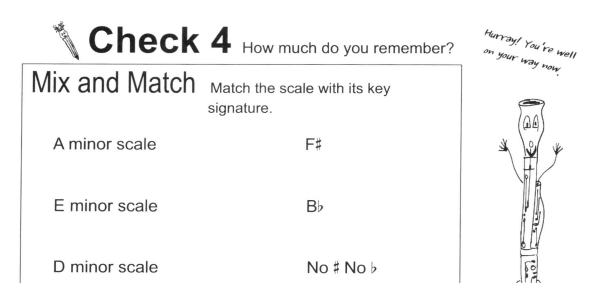

Mix and Match Match the scale with its key signature.

A minor scale   F♯

E minor scale   B♭

D minor scale   No ♯ No ♭

Quick Check Are the arpeggios correct? Tick or cross them.

A minor arpeggio   *G major arpeggio*   *F major arpeggio*

🎵 Quiz True or false? Circle the right answer.

1. A natural minor scale has exactly the same notes as C major scale.

        True   False

2. An octopus is an interval of eight notes.   True   False

3. Each minor scale shares a key signature with a major scale.   True   False

4. Arpeggios are made from the 1st, 3rd, 5th and 7th notes of a scale.

        True   False

5. D minor and F major share a key signature.   True   False

How many did you get right?

Musical Symbols

In music, symbols are used to show musical detail e.g. whether to play loud or quiet (dynamics) or how to tongue (articulation) and many others. Here are a few of the most commonly used.

gradually louder

gradually quieter

' Breath Mark (sometimes [∨] or √ are also used)

Slur –joined smoothly

Fermata - pause on the note

Phrase mark - showing one musical phrase

Accent – stressed

Staccato - short, detached

Tenuto - held and given a slight pressure

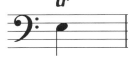

Trill- alternate rapidly to the note above

Musical Terms

Italian words are often used in music to show tempo (speed), dynamics (louds and softs) and directions. Many of them are abbreviated. Here are some of the most commonly used.

accelerando / accel. - *gradually faster*

adagio - *slow*

allegretto - *fairly fast (but not as fast as allegro)*

allegro - *fast*

andante - *at a medium (walking) speed*

crescendo / cresc. - *gradually louder*

da capo / D.C. - *repeat from the beginning*

dal segno / D.S. - *repeat from the sign*

decrescendo / decresc. - *gradually quieter*

diminuendo / dim. - *gradually quieter*

dolce - *sweetly*

fine - *the end*

f forte - *loud*

ff fortissimo - *very loud*

grazioso - *graceful*

largo - *slow, stately*

legato - *smoothly*

mezzo - *moderately*

mf / mezzo forte - *moderately loud*

mp / mezzo piano - *moderately quiet*

moderato - *moderately*

p / piano - *quiet*

pp / pianissimo - *very quiet*

presto - *fast*

rallentando / rall. - *gradually slower*

ritenuto / rit. - *held back*

tempo - *speed, time (a tempo - in time)*

vivace - *lively, fast*

Metronome Marking

♩ = **76**   *76 crotchets in a minute*

Rearrange these dynamic markings from quietest to loudest.

p   *f*   *mf*   *ff*   *pp*   *mp*

....

Join the term, abbreviation and symbol to its description.

rallentando   *gradually quieter*   *gradually louder*   crescendo

cresc.   rall.

accel.   accelerando

diminuendo   *gradually slower*   *gradually faster*   dim.

Write the symbol.

Staccato   Accent   Tenuto   Fermata

Add symbols and dynamics to this phrase of music. Be as creative as you like!

Write a phrase that changes tempo gradually.

Write a phrase that changes dynamic gradually.

Repeats and Directions

Repeat from the
beginning

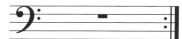

Repeat the
section

D.S. *Dal Segno* Repeat from the sign

𝄋 *Segno* Sign

D.S. al Coda Repeat from the sign and then play the Coda

⊕ *Coda* A coda is a phrase that ends a piece of music.

D.C. *Da Capo* Go back to the beginning

D.C. al Fine Go back to the beginning and play to Fine

First-time Bars and Second-time Bars

When a composer wants a tune to be repeated but with a different ending the second time, he or she might use First-time Bars and Second-time Bars instead of writing out the tune in full.

First-time ending

Second-time ending

Create a trail. Draw arrows to show where you go
and explain the dynamic markings in this piece.

Dizzy Demon
from our Demon Studies book

Chipper and dandy with the world spinning

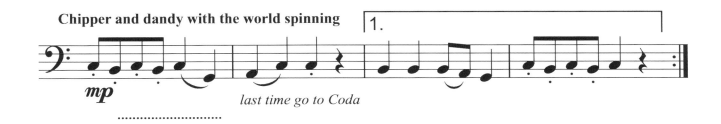

last time go to Coda

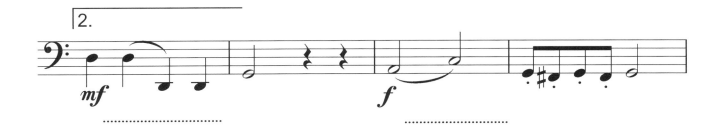

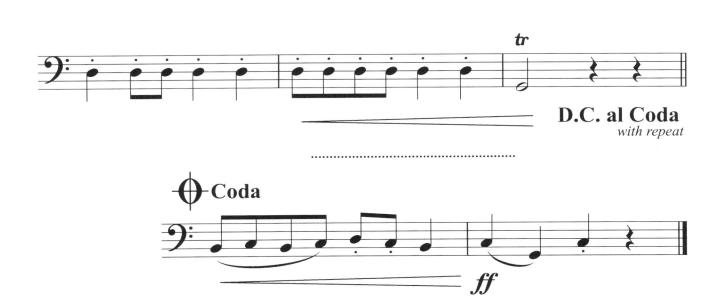

D.C. al Coda
with repeat

Coda

✏ Check 5 How much do you remember?

*Fantastic work!
You've nearly finished.
What a mover!*

Mix and Match Match the term with its definition.

D.S.	moderately loud
D.C.	gradually faster
pp	gradually quieter
mf	gradually slower
Allegro	at a medium (walking) speed
Andante	gradually louder
diminuendo	repeat from the beginning
crescendo	very quiet
rallentando	repeat from the sign
accelerando	quick

Quick Check Are the symbols correct? Tick or cross them.

Staccato   *Accent*   *Slur*   *Pause*   *Tenuto*

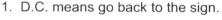

Quiz True or false? Circle the right answer.

1. D.C. means go back to the sign.   True   False

2. Trills move from the written note to the note below.   True   False

3. *Fine* means 'the beginning'.   True   False

4. An accent is shown by a little arrow.   True   False

5. A staccato note is shown by a dot.   True   False

6. First and Second-time Bars are different endings. True   False

7. D.S. means go back to the beginning.   True   False

How many did you get right?

The Bassoon

How well do you know your bassoon?

The Bore

Draw arrows to the parts of the bassoon.

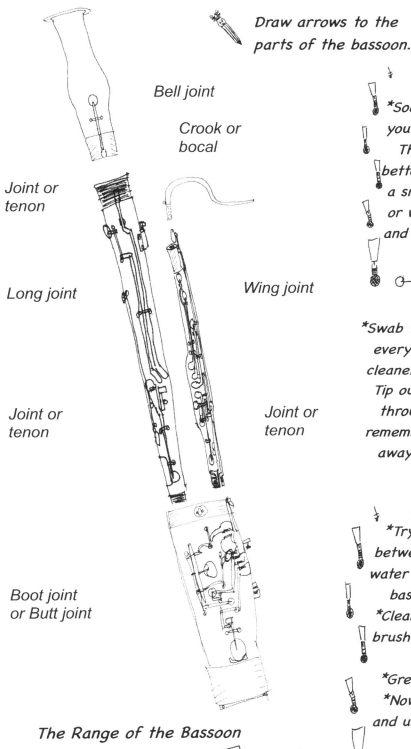

Bell joint

Crook or bocal

Joint or tenon

Long joint

Wing joint

Joint or tenon

Joint or tenon

Boot joint or Butt joint

Bassoon Care

*Soak your reed in water while you put your bassoon together. This will help the reed play better. Don't be tempted to have a sneaky drink or snack before or while playing, food particles and sugars do deadly damage to reeds and bassoons.

*Swab the wing and boot joints after every playing with a pull-through cleaner to remove debris and saliva. Tip out water from the boot joint through the wing joint hole and remember to keep your damp swabs away from the bassoon when its packed away.

*Try not to lay your bassoon flat between bouts of playing, otherwise water will soak into the pads and the bassoon will pop when you play.
*Clean your crook every 2 weeks by brushing through with a crook brush or swab.
*Grease the tenons if they're stiff.
*Now and then, polish the keywork and use a soft paintbrush to dust all the nooks and crannies.

The Range of the Bassoon

The Bassoon Family

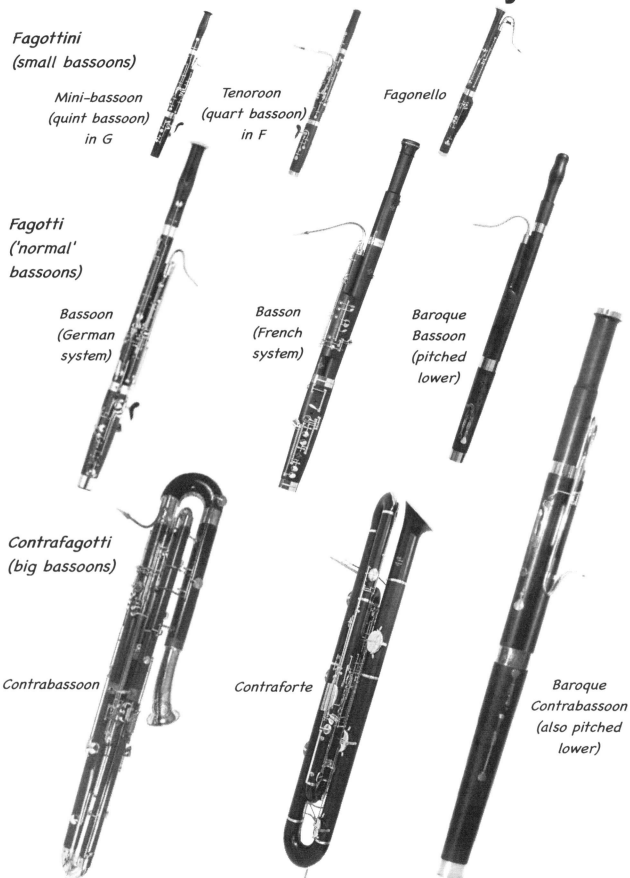

*Fagottini
(small bassoons)*

*Mini-bassoon
(quint bassoon)
in G*

*Tenoroon
(quart bassoon)
in F*

Fagonello

*Fagotti
('normal'
bassoons)*

*Bassoon
(German
system)*

*Basson
(French
system)*

*Baroque
Bassoon
(pitched
lower)*

*Contrafagotti
(big bassoons)*

Contrabassoon

Contraforte

*Baroque
Contrabassoon
(also pitched
lower)*

The Woodwind Family

Bassoons are the lowest members of the woodwind family.

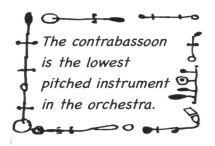

The contrabassoon is the lowest pitched instrument in the orchestra.

The oboe and cor anglais also use a double reed.

 Circle the instrument that is not a member of the woodwind family.

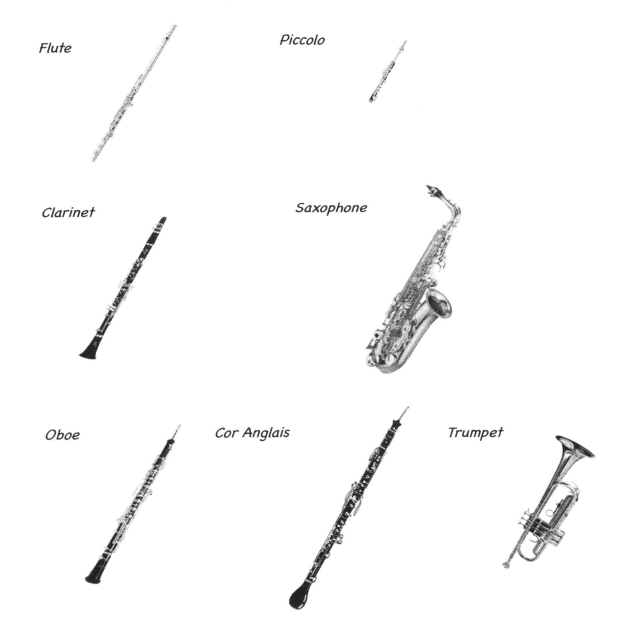

Flute

Piccolo

Clarinet

Saxophone

Oboe

Cor Anglais

Trumpet

Interesting Bassoon Facts

The bassoon is the only instrument in the orchestra that needs every finger and thumb to play notes.

The bassoon's four octave range means it has the largest range of notes of any woodwind instrument in the orchestra.

The Dulcian was the forerunner to the bassoon and was used until around 1700. It also had a double reed and a metal crook but was carved from a single piece of wood.

Many bassoons are made from Bosnian mountain maple or red maple from Canada

The Bocal is another name for the crook.

The Italian word for bassoon is 'fagotto' which means 'bundle of sticks'.

In the 1650s, Hotteterre, a French instrument maker, invented the 4 section bassoon and then makers began adding keywork and the Baroque Bassoon was born.

A reed that has stopped playing well, may just need a rest. Keep it in a safe place and try it again in a few weeks or months or years!

Arundo Donax (the plant used for reed cane) is like bamboo and is grown in plantations in places such as the south of France, Spain, Italy, Germany and in California.

German bassoons are played in most parts of the world and use the Heckel (or German) keywork system. French bassons, played mostly in France and Belgium, use the Buffet (or French) system which has different fingering and makes a different sound.

Final Check

Wordsearch

```
C D H Y A N D A N T E K I M D
O D N E C S E R C P T T P E L
C K G R A Z I O S O E G C O T
A O F S E V Z K T N O R M T V
B K D C V I P A U T E I L U I
O B L N W O C T A S S A O N V
F O R T E C O T C S R T M E A
D R I N A U R E I G T B I T C
A U X T A O N T O E E M S I E
L L S J P D R I R W A G S R Y
E S L E O O B G M R K M I P A
G C B E F T E P C I E P N I R
A L A B G L T A P Z D J A A W
T E S H L R T V Z T V N I N E
O F S A C O O O T S E R P O L
```

Can you find these words?

ALLEGRETTO
ALLEGRO
ANDANTE
BASS
CLEF
CRESCENDO
DECRESCENDO
DIMINUENDO
DOLCE
FORTE
FORTISSIMO
GRAZIOSO
LARGO

LEGATO
MEZZO
PIANO
PIANISSIMO
PRESTO
RITENUTO
SLUR
STACCATO
TENUTO
VIVACE

Can you find these words?

ARUNDODONAX
BAROQUE
BASSON
BASSOON
BELL
BOOTJOINT
CONTRABASSOON
CROOK
DULCIAN
FAGOTTO
HECKEL
KEYWORK
LONGJOINT
MAPLE
REED
SEATSTRAP
SLING
TENOROON
WINGJOINT

```
                          X B
                        F C A N
                      W A O S Q E
                    C B G N S C P L
                  B C A O T O M L B P
                H O D R T R O Z V H I   A
              D E O L O T A N Q C U Z O M
            N U C T O Q O B N O S S A B N U
          Q P L K J N U X A N O D O D N U R A
        O Q W C E O G E U S K W H L T N M L K Z
        D A K I L I J D P S E A A J T T W Z O E
          Z U A E N O E L O Y C S E W I H S B
            G N Y T I E L O W P N P N C E F
              N I R N R E N O O H G H A U
                I N T R B R R A J V T Q
                  L S N Z O K O R S C
                    S S O H I N T R
                      N C N I R O
                        T F A O
                          P K
```

Congratulations! You've finished. What an achievement. Why not visit the Wild Music website and check your amswers?

The Bassoonist's Progress

Tick the box for each topic completed.

☐ Bass Clef

☐ Letter Names

☐ Note Values

☐ Stems

☐ Rests

☐ Check 1

☐ Time Signatures

☐ Accidentals

☐ Quavers

☐ Ledger Lines

☐ Check 2

☐ Major Scales

☐ Key Signatures

☐ Dotted Crotchets

☐ Check 3

☐ Degrees of the Scale

☐ Intervals

☐ Minor Scales

☐ Arpeggios

☐ Check 4

☐ Musical Symbols

☐ Musical Terms

☐ Repeats and Directions

☐ Check 5

☐ The Bassoon

☐ The Bassoon Family

☐ The Woodwind Family

☐ Interesting Bassoon Facts

☐ Final Check

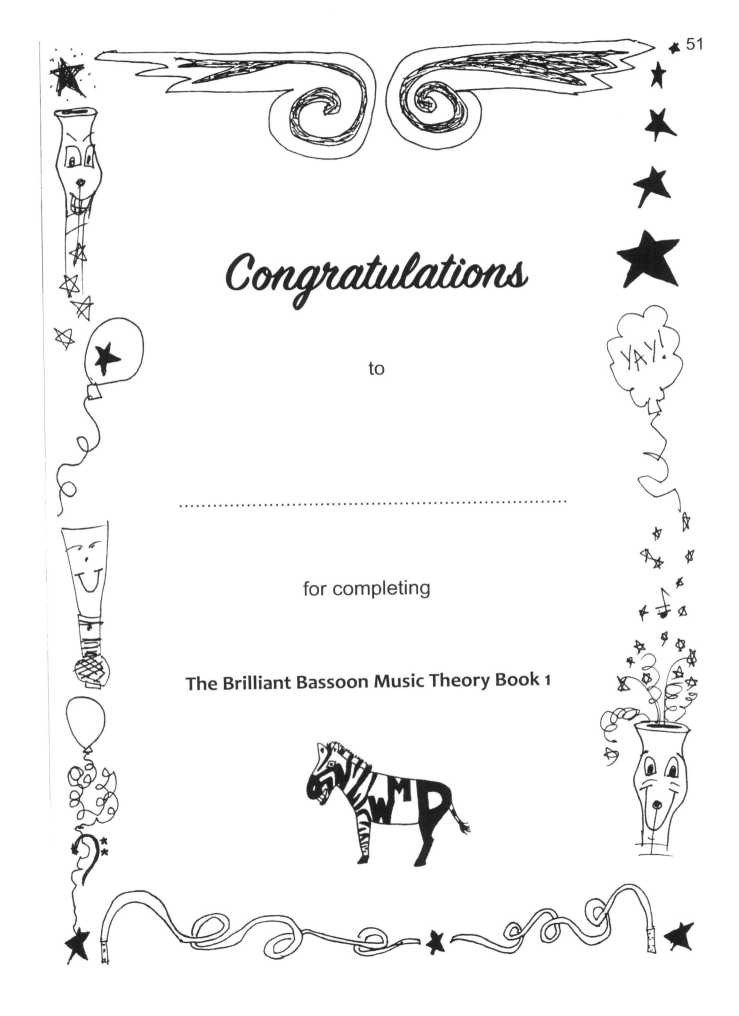

Congratulations

to

....

for completing

The Brilliant Bassoon Music Theory Book 1

If you have enjoyed **The Brilliant Bassoon Music Theory Book 1** why not try the other books in the **Brilliant Bassoon** series!

For more info, please visit: **WildMusicPublications.com**

All of our books are available to download, or you can order from Amazon.

Introducing some of our favourites:

50+ Greatest Classics

Moonlight and Roses

Christmas Carols

Trick or Treat – A Halloween Suite

Bassoon Practice Notebook

Fish 'n' Ships

Easy Duets from Around the World

Christmas Duets

Music Theory Book 2

Printed in Great Britain
by Amazon